Stories for Halloween

I Talk You Talk Press

CONTENTS

INTRODUCTION

The bus stopped at the Mount Washington Hotel in New Hampshire. Five people were waiting. They got on the bus, and it drove away. It was early evening, and it was snowing heavily.

"It usually takes three hours from here to Boston," said the bus driver. "But I think it will take longer because of the snow. We don't usually have snow at the end of October. Or if it does snow, it only snows a little. This big snow storm is unusual for this time of year."

They travelled for about two hours. Outside, the snow was falling. Everything was white. The people on the bus could not see the trees by the side of the road. The bus moved more and more slowly.

The driver was talking to his bus company in Boston. He was watching his GPS monitor carefully. Then he said, "I'm sorry, folks. We will have to stop for a while. This is called a whiteout. I can't see the road. I can't see if any car or bus is coming towards us. It is very dangerous. There is a roadside picnic area ahead. I will drive in there. We will wait until it stops snowing."

He drove the bus into the picnic area.

"How long will we have to wait?" asked a young woman with red hair.

"Maybe two hours," answered the driver. "Maybe longer. It will stop snowing in about two hours, but there will be a lot of snow on the ground. Maybe we will have to wait until the snow plough comes and moves the snow.

"Why don't you all come to the front of the bus? I have cookies and chocolate. I have a machine to heat water. I will make some

1

coffee."

The people moved to the front of the bus.

"Let's introduce ourselves," said one of the men. "I'm Charles Watt. I'm from Boston. I am in this area on business."

The young woman with red hair spoke next. "I'm Pamela. Pamela Morton. I went to visit my mother. She lives in Conway. I live in Boston too. I am a little worried about my son. He is staying with friends."

"Can't you call them?" asked Charles.

"I tried, but my cell phone isn't working. I guess there is no reception here in the forest."

"I'll send a message to my office," said the driver. "The office will contact your friends. Does anyone else want to send a message?"

"I'd like to send a message to my wife," said Charles. "I don't want her to worry."

The bus driver took the phone numbers and messages from Pamela and Charles, and spoke to his office.

"Now I will introduce myself," said the driver. "I'm Ben Silverman. I have been driving buses for more than thirty years."

"And I'm Stefan," said a young man. "I work with computers. I have been on a hiking vacation."

An older woman spoke next. "I'm Susan Swanson. I'm on vacation."

"Are you Irish?" asked Pamela.

Susan smiled. "Yes. I come from Dublin."

There was one more passenger. He was an old man. He was wearing a hat. He looked very happy and cheerful, but he didn't speak.

"And you are...?" asked the bus driver.

"Who?" answered the old man. "Oh, me? I'm sorry. I was thinking. I'm Jack. Everyone calls me Old Jack. I'm from England. I travel around collecting ghost stories. I was staying at the Mount Washington Hotel because they have a very interesting ghost there."

"Oh! Tonight is Halloween, so tell us the story!" said Susan.

Old Jack laughed. "No. I don't think I will tell you that story. I want to put it in my next book! But I will tell you another story. I think it is interesting."

1. OLD JACK'S STORY – THE BOY AND THE TOYS

"I travel around the world looking for ghost stories. Then I write books about them. I have heard many ghost stories in my life. I could tell you many stories about castles, hotels and pubs with ghosts, but I'd like to tell you a story about my family. When I was a young boy, I often visited my Aunt Edna in Edinburgh. I liked visiting my Aunt Edna. She lived in a big old house. She had a big garden. On sunny days I enjoyed playing in the garden because my house in England didn't have a garden. I climbed trees and played with the neighbour's cat. Aunt Edna's house had many rooms. The rooms were full of antiques and old things.

"I had no brothers or sisters, so I was always alone. Well, I was alone until one year…I was about eight or nine. In August, I went to Edinburgh for a month as usual. My mother and father didn't come. My father had to work. I went alone. I remember that summer very well. It rained every day while I was in Edinburgh. I couldn't play in the garden. Aunt Edna was old. She stayed in the living room, knitting, or listening to the radio. Sometimes her friends came to the house for tea. It was boring for me because I couldn't go outside.

"Aunt Edna felt sorry for me. 'Let me show you something,' she said.

"She took me upstairs. We went past the second floor. We went up to the third floor. She opened a small door. The room was empty. In one corner, there was a big cabinet. 'Look in the cabinet,' said Aunt Edna, and she went away.

"I opened the cabinet. There was a big box. I took the box out of the cabinet and put it in the middle of the room. It was very dusty. I wiped the dust off the lid, and opened it. The box was full of toys! There were soldier figures, ships, books, and other exciting things. I played with them all day.

"The next morning, I woke up and had breakfast. I talked with Aunt Edna for a while, and then I ran up the stairs to the room with the toy box. I opened the door and I was very shocked! There was a boy in the room! He was about nine years old. He was playing with my toys!

"I thought, *Aunt Edna didn't tell me another boy was here. Maybe he lives next door. Why didn't she tell me?*

"'Who are you?' I asked. He looked at me and smiled. 'I'm John.'

"'What are you doing here?' I asked.

"He looked at me and asked, 'What are you doing here?'

"'What?' I said. 'This is my aunt's house. I stay here every summer.'

"The boy smiled. 'I see.' Then he said, 'I live here.'

"I laughed. 'No you don't!'

"He didn't smile. 'I do!' he said.

"'OK,' I said. 'I'm going to ask Aunt Edna.' I turned around and walked to the stairs. 'Wait!' said the boy. 'If you don't say anything, I'll let you play with my toys.'

"I looked at him. 'Your toys? Are these your toys?'

"'Yes', he said.

"I thought, *Maybe he lives in the next house. Maybe Aunt Edna bought the toys for the local children. But why does she keep them in her house? Maybe she is lonely. Maybe she likes having children here. But why didn't she tell me?*

"The boy gave me a soldier. 'You can be this soldier. Let's have a battle!'

"I closed the door and sat down. We played for hours! It was so much fun! A few times, my Aunt Edna shouted, 'Young Jack! Don't be so noisy!' But she never shouted at John.

"We played all morning, until Aunt Edna shouted, 'Young Jack! It's lunchtime!'

"'Come on! It's lunchtime! Will you eat with us?' I asked the boy. He didn't say anything. Then, I stopped talking and looked carefully at the boy. He was wearing very old style clothes. I noticed a watch in his jacket pocket. It was an old style watch. Suddenly, I felt very frightened. I turned around and ran down the stairs. I screamed

'Aunt Edna! Aunt Edna! There's a boy! There's a boy!'

"Aunt Edna took me into the living room and sat next to me on the sofa. 'What happened, Young Jack?' she asked.

"'There was a boy…the toys...he had old clothes and…'

"Aunt Edna laughed. 'You have a good imagination Young Jack. You have no brothers or sisters. I'm sure you are lonely.'

"'It's true! I saw him!' I said. 'We played together!'

"'I heard you shouting and laughing, but I didn't hear another voice,' said Aunt Edna.

"'But he was shouting and laughing too!' I said.

"Aunt Edna stood up. 'Come on,' she said. 'Let's go to the toy room together.'

"We went up the stairs. I was very frightened. Aunt Edna opened the door.

"'See! There is no one here!' she said. There was no one in the room.

"'But, but, Aunt Edna, I saw a boy!' I said.

"'OK, Young Jack. It's OK.' Aunt Edna put her arms around me. 'It's OK.' Then, she said, 'Did the boy tell you his name?'

"'Yes, his name was John!' I said. Aunt Edna looked at me for a few seconds.

"'What is it?' I asked.

"'Let's go down to the living room,' she said.

"We went into the living room and she took an old photograph album from the bookcase. She opened it and pointed to a picture.

"'Is this the boy?' she asked. In the photograph, there was a family. A mother, father and two young boys. One of the boys was John. 'Yes! That's him!' I said. 'Who is he?'

"Aunt Edna smiled. 'John was my father's brother. He died before I was born. He was only eight years old. He was a very sick boy. The doctor couldn't help him.'

"'But if he is dead, why is he here?' I asked. 'I don't understand!'

"Aunt Edna said, 'I don't know. But maybe you shouldn't play with his toys anymore. The toys in the box were John's toys.' She looked at the clock. 'We'll go shopping after lunch. I'll buy you some new toys.'

"Aunt Edna went to the room at the top of the house. She put the toys in the box and closed the door.

"After lunch we went shopping and Aunt Edna bought me many

new toys. I was very happy to get new toys. I played with them in my bedroom. I felt frightened in the house for a few days. But I never saw the boy again.

"I stayed with Aunt Edna for another few weeks. On my last morning there, I woke up and turned to look at the clock next to my bed. On the table, there was a watch. It was an old style watch. *What's this?* I thought. I picked it up and looked at it. On the back of the watch, I could see some letters. I looked very carefully. ---*John*---

"It was John's watch! After that, I became very interested in ghosts and ghost stories."

Everyone on the bus was very surprised.

"Is it really true?" asked Stefan. "Was there really a watch?"

Old Jack smiled and put his hand in his pocket. He took out an old watch and passed it to Stefan. "Here, take a look! What do you think?"

Stefan turned the watch over and read the name. ---*John*---

He smiled. "Yes, I think it is true."

2. STEFAN'S STORY – THE GIRL WITH NO EYES

"I hope you liked my story. I think it was a good story for Halloween. Does anyone else have a ghost story?" asked Old Jack.

"I can tell you a story," said Stefan. "It's not a ghost story, but it's scary. Would you like to hear it?"

"Yes, please!" said everyone.

"My family came from Romania, but I was born in the USA and grew up here. Maybe you know that there are many legends in Romania about vampires and werewolves. Of course, these are just stories. But Romania is a very special place, and unusual things happen there.

"A few years ago, I went on vacation to Romania. I went to stay with my great-uncle and his family in the mountains. It was a very beautiful place. The village was very small. There were only a few houses. It was very quiet and lonely. I like cycling, so I often went out into the forest on my bicycle.

"One day, I rode down a small side road in the forest. I passed some old buildings. One building looked like a church. Other buildings looked like houses. No one was living there. The buildings were all falling down.

"*This was a village,* I thought. *No one lives here now. I wonder why?*

"It was a beautiful day, so I continued riding. On the road, just past the village, I saw two people walking along the road. I rode towards them. It was a young girl and a very old woman. The girl was singing. She was carrying some flowers in one hand. The old woman was holding the girl's other hand. She seemed to be leading her.

"I cannot speak Romanian well, but I can speak a little. When I got closer to the woman and the girl, I opened my mouth to say 'buna ziua'. That means hello or good afternoon. But the words did not come out of my mouth. I looked at the young girl. She had beautiful black hair and a smiling mouth, but … she had no eyes!

"It was a shock. Above her nose, there was nothing. Just smooth skin. I rode past them very quickly. *What a terrible thing!* I thought. *That poor girl.*

"I stopped a few hundred metres up the road and looked back. I couldn't see the girl or the old woman. *Maybe they went into that old, empty village,* I thought.

"I rode back to my great-uncle's house. When I rode past the village, I looked for the young girl and the old woman but I didn't see anyone.

"That night at dinner, I told my relatives about my cycle ride. 'I saw something very sad,' I said. 'I passed a young girl. She was singing and she was carrying flowers. She seemed very happy. But she had no eyes. Do you know her?'

"My great-aunt screamed. She ran out of the house. Everyone else stopped eating. They looked at me.

"'What is wrong?' I asked. 'What did I say?'

"My cousin was also visiting. He was born in the village, but then he moved to Bucharest. He spoke good English, so I could talk to him easily.

"'Where did you see the girl?' asked my cousin.

"'There was an old village in the forest. No one was living there. She was walking down the road near that village. A very old woman was with her,' I answered.

"My cousin looked very serious.

"'You know there are many legends in Romania,' he said. 'I don't believe the old stories, but many people here believe them. This area has its own stories and legends. One of the stories is about the girl with no eyes. I will tell you the story. Long ago, there was a strigoaica living in the village in the forest.'

"'Sorry, what is a strigoaica?' I asked.

"'I think in English it is a vampire,' answered my cousin. 'A female vampire. Her name was Elena. The local people realised that Elena was a vampire, and they planned to kill her. The men from the village went to her house. Elena was waiting for them. She said, 'You are blind. You are stupid. You think if you kill me, I will disappear. But that is not true. You can kill me, but I will always be here.'

"'The village men laughed at Elena. They took her away from her house, and before they killed her, they took out her eyes.

"'Now we will see who is blind!' they said, laughing.

"'As Elena was dying, she said, 'Every girl born in this village will be blind. You will see your beautiful daughters, but they will never see you. And all these girls with no eyes will be vampires. Then you will remember me!'

"'The men cut off Elena's head. They filled the mouth of the head with garlic, and they buried her.

"'For a few months after that, life in the village was normal. But then a woman in the village gave birth to a daughter. She was a beautiful baby but she had no eyes. The people in the village were very frightened. They ran away. They didn't take the baby girl with no eyes. But the baby's great-grandmother stayed with her.' My cousin stopped speaking.

"'It is a terrible story,' I said. 'Did I see ghosts today? Did I see the ghost of the girl and her great-grandmother?'

"'No. People in this village believe that the girl and her great-grandmother became vampires. They never died. People say that if anyone sees the vampires, someone in their family will die,' said my cousin.

"'Oh, really? People don't believe that now! It is just an old story,' I said.

"'Maybe,' said my cousin. He looked around the table. 'But my family believe it.'"

Stefan stopped talking. Everyone on the bus looked at him.

"That is a great story," said Charles. "It is amazing that people believe these old stories."

Stefan spoke very quietly. "I believe this old story."

"Why?" Everyone on the bus was very surprised.

"I believe in it, because that night, my cousin died. I went to look at his dead body. He had no eyes, and no one ever found them."

3. CHARLES' STORY – THE HAUNTED HOUSE

Everyone on the bus was very quiet. Stefan's story was very scary. Then Charles said, "I will tell you a story. It is not so scary, but it is about ghosts."

"I told you I am in northern New Hampshire on business. My company buys and sells old books. I travel to many places looking for books.

"A few years ago, my boss sent me to England. A family called Faddenborough lived in a big old house in North Yorkshire. They wanted to sell some books. The house was very far from any town, so the family invited me to stay in their house while I looked at the books.

"I flew to Manchester. I rented a car and drove to the house. It was a beautiful old house with very pretty gardens. Mrs Faddenborough met me at the door.

"'Come in,' she said. 'You are in time for lunch.'

"I ate lunch with Mr and Mrs Faddenborough. Then Mrs Faddenborough showed me to my bedroom. It was a large room with a fireplace and a big desk in the corner. 'Wow,' I said. 'This room is wonderful.'

"Mrs Faddenborough smiled. 'I hope you will be comfortable,' she said. 'Sometimes this room is very noisy.'

"'I am sure I will sleep very well,' I said. 'I would like to start work now. Can you show me the library?'

"'Yes. Of course,' she said.

"She took me to the library. There were thousands of books. 'We

10

have so many books. Some are valuable, and some are not. We hope you will find some very valuable books and buy them. The roof of this house leaks, and we want money to fix it.' Mrs Faddenborough smiled and went away.

"I found a table in the middle of the library. I set up my computer and my notebooks. Then I started working. I looked at every shelf of books. If I saw anything interesting, I put it on the table. When I had a few books on the table, I sat down and looked at them closely. I took notes and checked the databases on my computer.

"After about two hours, I heard noises. *Someone is in the library,* I thought. *Maybe it is Mr Faddenborough, or maybe another member of the family.*

"I continued working. Then a strange thing happened. I felt there was someone standing on the other side of the table. I looked up, but there was no one there. But the air seemed a little misty. Next, the books on the table moved up into the air and fell down onto the floor.

"I jumped up. Then the misty air came towards me. I felt very cold. I was shivering. The door of the library opened. Mrs Faddenborough walked in. 'Is everything OK?' she asked. 'Do you have everything you need?'

"I couldn't answer. I was too shocked and cold. Mrs Faddenborough looked at me. 'Are you ill?' she asked.

"'I feel very cold,' I said. I pointed to the books on the floor. 'These books flew into the air and fell onto the floor.'

"Mrs Faddenborough sighed. 'I am very angry with my husband. He never remembers to do anything!'

"I was puzzled. 'Did your husband do this?' I asked.

"'No. Uncle George did that!' said Mrs Faddenborough. 'I told my husband to tell Uncle George that you were coming. Come and have a cup of coffee. I will talk to my husband. He must talk to Uncle George.'

"I followed Mrs Faddenborough to the kitchen. She turned on the coffee maker, and disappeared. Very soon she came back. 'My husband is talking to Uncle George now. I am sorry Uncle George shocked you. He loves the library. Most of the books are his. He bought them many years ago.'

"'I must talk to him,' I said. 'I am sure he can tell me about the books. It will save a lot of time.'

"'Uncle George doesn't talk, but he writes notes sometimes. I am sure he wants the roof fixed. So maybe he will help you.'

"When I finished my coffee, I went back to the library. The books from the floor were back on the table. Next to them, was another book. It was very old. On top of the book was a note. I read the note:

---*Look at this one.*---

"I opened the book very carefully. I was excited. It was a very rare and valuable book. I wrapped the book carefully in special paper and started making notes on my computer. Soon it was dark. I went to eat dinner with Mr and Mrs Faddenborough. 'Uncle George left a very valuable and interesting book on my work table. I want to thank him. Can I meet him please? Does he live here in the house?' I asked.

"Mr Faddenborough put down his knife and fork, and looked at me. 'Uncle George has been dead for forty years,' he said. 'His ghost stays in the library. I told Uncle George's ghost to help you. I am pleased he found a good book for you.'

"'You have a ghost in this house?' I asked.

"Mrs Faddenborough laughed. 'We have many ghosts in this house. Usually Uncle George is very polite. He is usually invisible. Some of the other ghosts are very rude. There is Great Great Great Grandmother Sylvia. She likes to turn taps on. The problem is, she never turns the taps off again. We often have floods in the bathrooms. And there is the soldier. You can see him. He wears a uniform and carries a sword. He is very annoying too. He likes to walk up and down the hallway. He makes a lot of noise at night. And the woman in grey. You can see her too. She wears a grey dress. She cries all the time. I try to talk to her. I ask her if I can help. But she never answers me. We don't know who she is, or where she comes from.'

"'Did you tell Mr Watt about Bessy?' asked Mr Faddenborough. 'I am sure Bessy will visit him.'

"'Bessy?' I asked. I was thinking that Mr and Mrs Faddenborough were crazy.

"'Oh, yes,' said Mrs Faddenborough. 'Bessy. Bessy is sometimes a very naughty ghost. A long time ago, Bessy was a maid here. The master of the house fell in love with her, but then he killed her. The problem is that Bessy's ghost still likes men. We think she is looking for a boyfriend. When a man stays here, her ghost is always in his bedroom. She laughs and touches things. I hope she will not keep you awake!'

"'I think you can hire people to come to your house,' I said. 'These people can stop ghosts.'

"Mr Faddenborough looked surprised. 'But we don't want to do that,' he said.

"'Oh, no,' said his wife. 'We have no neighbours and the nearest town is far away. The ghosts are like friends to us.'

"I stayed in the house for a few days. Uncle George's ghost helped me a lot. He found many good books for me to buy. One day, I found a very interesting book. I was sitting at the table looking at it when I felt cold air around me. A pencil on the desk moved into the air and wrote on a piece of paper:

--- *Not that one.* ---

"'Oh,' I said. 'I understand. You want to keep that one.'

"The pencil wrote again:

--- *Yes.*---

"I liked Uncle George's ghost but I didn't like the other ghosts. Bessy's ghost touched my hair when I was in bed. She laughed all the time. She played with my hairbrush and toothbrush. It was very difficult to sleep. The soldier marched up and down the hallway ...*bang, bang, bang*... the noise continued all night. Sometimes I heard the woman in grey. It was a very unusual house.

"I was not frightened. Maybe you think that is strange. I think I was not frightened because Mr and Mrs Faddenborough were nice people. They thought the ghosts were normal. The ghosts were like their family.

"Soon it was time for me to leave. I bought some books from Mr and Mrs Faddenborough. They were very valuable books. I gave them a cheque for a lot of money. They were very happy. They had enough money to fix the roof.

"As I drove away, I saw Uncle George's ghost for the first and last time. He was standing at the library window. He was smiling and waving to me."

4. PAMELA'S STORY – A SPECIAL PUMPKIN

"I love that story," said Pamela. "Uncle George's ghost is not very scary, but some ghosts are very frightening. I saw one last year.

"My son Jarrod was eight years old. One day at the end of May, Jarrod came home from school as usual. He ran into the house shouting, 'Mom! Mom! Can we plant pumpkins for Halloween?'

"I was in the kitchen. 'Pumpkins for Halloween?' I asked.

"'Yes, Mom. If we want pumpkins for Halloween we have to plant the seeds now!'

"'Uh, yes. I guess so,' I answered. 'I will go to the garden shop and buy some seeds.'

"'No, Mom! It's OK! I have a seed.'

"Jarrod put his hand into the pocket of his jeans. He showed me a pumpkin seed.

"'Where did you get that?' I asked.

"'I met an old man on the way home from school. He gave it to me.'

"'Jarrod!' I shouted. 'You are not allowed to talk to strangers!'

"'Oh, Mom,' said Jarrod. 'He was a nice old man. He said, 'Do you know about Halloween? Do you know how to grow pumpkins?' He gave me this seed.'

"'Well, OK,' I said. 'But you must not talk to him again.'

"Jarrod put the seed on the kitchen counter. 'Please, Mom. Can we plant it?'

"'Yes, OK,' I said. 'But I will also buy some seeds from the garden shop.'

"The next Saturday, Jarrod and I went into the garden. We planted the seeds from the garden shop, and the seed from the old man.

"'I am going to put a special marker next to the old man's seed,' said Jarrod. 'I think this seed will grow into a very special pumpkin.'

"Jarrod took a plastic marker from the garage. He wrote 'Special Pumpkin' on the marker. He put it in the ground next to the seed from the old man.

"After ten days, there were two green leaves above the ground. They came from the special pumpkin seed. The other seeds had no leaves.

"'Oh, dear,' I said to Jarrod. 'The seeds from the garden shop were no good. I will buy some more.'

"I bought more seeds and planted them. But nothing happened.

"Jarrod said, 'I don't think the special pumpkin likes other pumpkins. That's why the other seeds cannot grow.'

"'Jarrod! Don't be so silly!' I said.

"The plant from the special seed grew very well. But usually, a pumpkin plant will grow many pumpkins. This plant had only one pumpkin.

"'Look! It's so big!' said Jarrod. 'It is still growing! I think it will be a monster pumpkin!'

"In late September, Jarrod spent a lot of time in the garden. One afternoon, his friend Karl called him. I went to the garden to tell him.

"I found Jarrod sitting on the ground next to the pumpkin plant.

"'Jarrod! Karl called. He is on the telephone. He wants you to go to eat pizza, and go to a movie with him,' I said.

"Jarrod looked up at me. 'Oh, I can't go. I'm busy!'

"'Busy?' I asked. 'What are you doing?'

"'I'm talking to the pumpkin. The pumpkin likes me to talk to it.'

"I looked at Jarrod. He looked tired.

"'Jarrod? Are you OK?' I asked.

"'I'm fine,' said Jarrod. 'I'm a little tired, but I'm OK.'

"'Come and talk to Karl,' I said.

"'No, Mom. You talk to him. Tell him I'm busy.'

"I went back into the house. I talked to Karl. I was worried. When we were eating dinner that night, I asked Jarrod, 'Have you seen the old man again? The man who gave you the pumpkin seed?'

"'In June and July, I often saw him.'

"'Jarrod! I told you not to speak to him!'

"'I didn't speak to him. You told me not to. He smiled and waved to me, and I waved back. But I never talked to him again.'

"'Do you see him now?' I asked.

"'No. I haven't seen him for a long time.'

"The next day, Jarrod was sick. 'I feel too tired to go to school,' he said.

"'OK. I will take you to see the doctor,' I said.

"Jarrod and I went to see the doctor. 'Jarrod is tired,' said the doctor. 'But he seems to be quite well. I don't think there is anything wrong. If he rests, he will feel better soon.'

"But Jarrod did not feel better. Every day he was very tired. He ate a lot. He was always hungry, but he lost a lot of weight. I was very worried. We went to the doctor many times. The doctor did tests. He sent Jarrod to a big hospital for more tests.

"All the doctors said the same thing. 'Jarrod is very tired, and he is losing weight. But we cannot find any illness.'

"Jarrod didn't want to watch television, or read, or talk to his friends. He only wanted to sit on the ground next to the pumpkin plant and talk to the pumpkin.

"I was very worried. I called the doctor and told him. 'What is the problem?' asked the doctor. 'He is outside in the fresh air. A pumpkin can't hurt him!'

"In the third week of October, Jarrod said, 'It's time to cut the pumpkin. It will not grow any more. It must dry, so we can make a face on the pumpkin for Halloween.'

"We went out into the garden to cut the pumpkin. Jarrod was very weak. He couldn't help me. The pumpkin was very big. I cut the pumpkin away from the plant. I got a wheelbarrow and I took the pumpkin to the garage. I unlocked the garage and took the pumpkin in. Then I locked the garage again. 'It can dry in here,' I said.

"The next week, Jarrod seemed a little better. He was not so tired. He had more energy. After a few days, he went back to school. On October thirtieth, he went to Karl's house to play. He called me just before dinnertime. 'Hey Mom,' he said. 'Karl has a great new video game. Can I stay here and eat dinner? Karl's mom said I can sleep over too.'

"I was pleased. *He's forgotten about that pumpkin. He is back to normal,* I thought.

"I ate dinner alone. After dinner I went into the living room to watch TV. But I kept thinking about the pumpkin. *I must make a face on the pumpkin,* I thought. *Tomorrow is Halloween. Jarrod will remember the pumpkin tomorrow.*

"The pumpkin was too big to carry into the kitchen. I took a knife, a big spoon and a garbage bag down to the garage. I turned the light on and started working. I cut the top off the pumpkin, and took all the flesh and seeds out. Then I cut triangles for the eyes and nose, and I cut out the mouth. It took a long time, but finally, I finished.

"The next day was Saturday. Karl's mother drove Jarrod home at about ten am. 'Jarrod and Karl want to go trick or treating tonight,' she said. 'I have a meeting so I can't go with them. Can you take them?'

"'Sure,' I said.

"'Great! Thank you. I will bring Karl here at about five thirty. Is that OK?'

"'No problem,' I said.

"Karl's mother drove away

"'Mom! Mom! I don't have a costume for trick or treat! I want to dress up as Mario from the video game!' said Jarrod.

It took all day to make a costume for Jarrod. He was very excited. He didn't ask about the pumpkin.

"At five thirty, Karl arrived. He was dressed as Luigi. Then Jarrod suddenly remembered the pumpkin. 'I want to show Karl the giant pumpkin,' he said. 'Did you make the face?'

"'Yes,' I said. 'I made a face on the pumpkin last night.'

"The two boys and I went down to the garage and I unlocked the door. The pumpkin was not in the wheelbarrow! It was on the floor!

"'What!' I shouted. When I spoke, the pumpkin seemed to move. It rolled around, and we could see the face.

"'Oh, hello!' said Jarrod. 'This is my friend Karl.'

"I looked and looked. When I left the garage the night before, the pumpkin had a simple face – two triangles for eyes, a triangle for a nose, and a mouth shape. Now the pumpkin had the face of a human!

"'Karl,' said Jarrod. 'This is the old man. He gave me the pumpkin seed.'

"'Hi,' said Karl.

"I was very frightened. I took Jarrod's hand and Karl's hand. I pulled them out of the garage. 'We have to hurry, or we will be late

17

for trick or treat,' I said. 'Go and get your bags for the candy. They are in the kitchen.'

"The two little boys ran back to the house and I closed the garage door and locked it.

"I was shaking. *What is happening?* I thought. I took the boys out to the street. We met the other parents and children.

"Karl and Jarrod had a great time playing trick or treat. After trick or treat, there was a neighbourhood party for the children. The children ate barbecue sausages and baked potatoes. They played games. At eight thirty, I took Karl and Jarrod back to my house.

"Karl's mother soon came and took him home. Jarrod fell asleep on the sofa. I picked him up and carried him to his room.

"*He can sleep in his Mario costume tonight,* I thought. I went back to the living room to watch TV, but I couldn't relax. *Was it my imagination? Did I imagine the face?* I read a book, and did a crossword puzzle, but I couldn't forget the pumpkin. It was almost midnight when I gave up. *I will have to go and look at that pumpkin again,* I thought.

"I went to Jarrod's bedroom to check that he was OK. He was asleep. His bag of Halloween candy was on the table next to his bed.

"I took a flashlight and the keys to the garage. I went outside. As I walked towards the garage I saw a dark shape. I stopped. *What is that?* I thought.

"I pointed the torch towards the shape. It was the wheelbarrow. And inside the wheelbarrow was the pumpkin!

"I moved the flashlight so I could see the pumpkin's face - three triangles and a mouth. It was a normal pumpkin face.

"*Maybe I am crazy,* I thought. *I was so worried about Jarrod, that I started imagining things.*

"Just then I saw another face. It was the old man's face. It was floating in the air above the pumpkin. It was white, and looked like smoke. Then I heard a voice. It was coming from the ghostly face hanging in the air.

"'I'm sorry I used your son. I hope you understand. I was dying. I wanted to live a little while longer. I always liked Halloween. The children are always so happy. I wanted to see the children at Halloween one more time. I'm going now. Goodbye.'

"Then, the face disappeared."

5. SUSAN'S STORY – THE FLOWERS ON THE STAIRS

"That sounds very scary," said Susan to Pamela. "Did your son ever ask about the pumpkin?"

"No," said Pamela. "Jarrod never talked about the old man or the pumpkin again. Do you have a ghost story, Susan?"

"Yes," said Susan. "I once had a very strange experience. A long time ago, I lived in a house near a river. The house was new. It had two bedrooms and a nice garden. I lived alone, with my pet poodle, Bob.

"It was about nine pm on Saturday night. I was sitting in the living room watching TV. Bob was sitting next to me. He was asleep. Suddenly, I heard a noise on the stairs. Bob jumped up. He heard it too. 'What was that?' I said to Bob.

"Bob started to growl. 'Grrr! Grrr!'

"I switched the TV off and listened carefully. There were footsteps on the stairs! Someone was in my house!

"Bob started to bark loudly and he ran to the door. I was very frightened. I picked up a glass vase of flowers. I took the flowers out of the vase. I opened the window and poured the water out. *If anyone attacks me, I will hit them with this vase,* I thought.

"Slowly, I opened the living room door, and Bob ran to the stairs. I switched on the light. There was no one there. But Bob was acting very strangely. He was looking at the stairs, and he was shaking and crying. He looked very frightened. 'What is it Bob?' I asked. He was looking at something in the middle of the stairs. He could see something. But I couldn't see anything strange.

"I walked up the stairs and looked in the rooms upstairs. There was no one there. Bob didn't come upstairs. He stayed at the bottom of the stairs, shaking.

"I looked in the bathroom and kitchen, but there was no one there. I filled the vase with water and went back into the living room. I put the flowers back into the vase and put the vase back on the table. I switched the TV on again. All night, Bob sat next to the living room door, crying. *What is it?* I thought. *Is it a ghost?* I was frightened, because I couldn't understand it.

"The next day, I went for a run along the river. It was a beautiful sunny day, but it was cold. When I left the house, Bob was asleep on the sofa. I ran for two hours.

"While I was running, I thought about the strange footsteps on the stairs, and Bob.

Was it a ghost? I thought. *No, there can't be a ghost. The house, and all the other houses here, are new. Ghosts don't live in new houses.*

"After my run, I walked back to my house. I opened the door. Bob usually came to the door. He was usually happy to see me. But, this time, the house was quiet.

"'Bob?' I said. 'Where are you?'

"I went inside. 'Aaaggh!' I screamed. I was so shocked, I couldn't move.

"On each step of the stairs, there was a flower. The flowers were from the vase in my living room. There were ten steps and ten flowers. At the top of the stairs I could see Bob. He looked happy. His eyes were closed and his tail was moving.

"'Bob! Bob!' I shouted. Bob didn't come down the stairs. 'Can't you hear me Bob?' I shouted.

"I was very frightened. I couldn't stay in my house. I took my car keys, closed the door and ran to my car.

"At that time, I was working in the local library. I drove there, parked my car and ran in.

"'Susan! What is it?' said Jill, my old boss.

"Jill took me into the staff room and gave me a hot cup of tea. I felt better. I told her the story.

"'Is it a ghost? It can't be a ghost!' I said. 'Ghosts don't come to new houses!'

"She listened carefully, and then she said, 'Wait a minute'. She went to the local history room of the library, and came back with a book.

"She opened it to a page. The page had a map of the town and some photographs.

"She pointed to the map. 'This map is from a hundred years ago. Here is the river. There is a girls' school here next to the river. The school closed about forty years ago. Then around five years ago, a housing company bought the land. They knocked the school down, and built houses on the old school land. Your house is one of those houses.'

"She turned to another page. It had a newspaper report from nineteen thirty.

"'Look at this,' she said. I read the newspaper report. One day, there was a fire in the school. The girls were very frightened and ran down the school stairs very quickly. Some of the girls fell down the stairs. One of the girls, an eight year old called Matilda, hit her head on the floor and died. Everyone was very shocked and upset. Her teacher at the time said, 'Matilda was a lively girl. She had many friends and she enjoyed playing very much.'

"'And look at this,' said Jill. She showed me another newspaper article from nineteen thirty two.

"After the accident, many of the schoolgirls saw the ghost of Matilda. The girls were very frightened. Some girls saw Matilda on the stairs. Others saw her at the classroom window. She often waved to the girls. So the teachers put flowers at the bottom of the stairs. After that, the ghost of Matilda did not come back.

"I looked at Jill. 'Do you think Matilda is in my house?' I asked.

"'Maybe,' said Jill. 'But don't be frightened. She is only a young girl. She won't hurt you or Bob. I think she wants to play with Bob.'

"'It's a sad story,' I said. I finished my tea. Then, I went to the flower shop. I bought a beautiful bunch of flowers. On the card with the flowers, I wrote:

---*To Matilda*---.

"Then, I went home. I opened the front door. Bob was waiting for me. He seemed happy to see me. I looked at the stairs. The flowers were still there. I picked each flower up and put them in the vase in the living room. Then, I put the new flowers in a different vase, and put the vase and the card on the table at the bottom of the stairs.

"I had a shower, and spent the afternoon doing the housework. Around five pm, I got changed. I planned to have dinner with my friends at a restaurant in town.

"'Be a good boy, Bob. I'll see you later,' I said to Bob. He ran upstairs. When I left the house, he usually ran to my bedroom window to watch me go out.

"I closed the door and looked up at the window to wave to Bob. It was nearly dark outside, but I could see a young girl in the window. She was wearing old-fashioned clothes. She was holding Bob, and she was smiling and waving at me. I smiled and waved back at her.

"After that, I bought new flowers for the vase at the bottom of the stairs every few weeks. I never saw Matilda again. Bob didn't see her again either."

6. THE DRIVER'S STORY – THE OLD MAN AT THE BUS STOP

"You have all told us a story," said the bus driver. "I guess it is my turn. I think we can leave here soon. But maybe there is enough time for you to listen to my story."

"Oh, yes please," said Old Jack.

"I was driving the last bus of the night. It was a cold rainy night, and I was driving to a small town, near Boston. I didn't know the area very well. I lived in a town about ten miles away, and it was only my second day on that bus route. There were only three passengers on the bus. There was a young man sitting at the back. He was listening to music on his earphones. There was a woman sitting in the middle. And there was another man near the front.

"It was about ten thirty, and we were driving along a dark country road. It was raining heavily, and I was looking forward to finishing work and going home. We were about a mile from the town. Ahead I could see a man standing at the bus stop. He was very old. *It is unusual to see a very old man out at this time,* I thought.

"I stopped the bus, and the bus doors opened. The wind was very strong and the rain came in through the open doors. The old man climbed up the steps very slowly. He was wearing a long red coat and black pants. He had a yellow baseball cap on. He took his bus pass out of his pocket and showed it to me. I said, 'Thanks'. The old man didn't look at me. I closed the door and waited for him to sit down. *He's taking a long time,* I thought. I watched in my mirror. Then, something strange happened. The man disappeared!

"The woman started screaming. The young man at the back of the bus jumped up. 'What happened? Where is he?!' he shouted.

"I stood up and walked to the middle of the bus. 'Where did he go? Where did he go?' I asked.

"The man at the front of the bus couldn't speak. He was so frightened, he couldn't move. The woman was shaking her head. 'He just…he just…disappeared!' she said.

"The young man ran past me and started hitting the door. 'Let me off! Let me off!' he shouted. 'I can't stay on this bus!'

"'Relax! It's OK,' I said. But the man was too frightened. 'Let me off!' He was hitting the doors very hard, so I opened the doors and he ran away into the dark night. I looked at the man and the woman. 'Let's go,' I said.

"I drove to the town and the man and the woman got off the bus. They said, 'Thank you', but they didn't say anything else. They were both still very shocked. So then I was alone. I had to take the bus back to the office. I locked the doors and drove through the dark streets to the office. I looked in my mirror every few seconds. I was worried the old man might come back. He didn't come back. I checked the bus and locked it. Then I went into the office. Richard, another bus driver was there.

"'What's the matter?' he asked. 'You look like you have seen a ghost!'

"'I have seen a ghost!' I said. I told him the story. He listened for a while. Then, he said, 'A red coat? And a yellow baseball cap? Ten thirty? About a mile from the town? I don't believe it! That sounds like William Vogel! But it can't be! No, I don't believe it!'

"'Who's William Vogel?' I asked.

"'He was a retired school teacher. He lived in the town. His daughter lived just outside the town. Every Tuesday, he went to her house for dinner. He always took the last bus. All the drivers knew him. Last year, I was driving your bus. One Tuesday, I was very surprised because he wasn't at the bus stop. The next day, I heard the news. He died that Tuesday evening when he was walking to the bus stop from his daughter's house. He had a heart attack. The next morning, his daughter found him dead in a field near the bus stop. I felt bad. Why didn't I see him? Why didn't I tell someone he wasn't at the bus stop?'

"'But you didn't know. You shouldn't feel bad,' I said. 'But it's strange. Why did his ghost come back? Why did he get on the bus? Why tonight?'

"'I don't know,' said Richard. He looked at the calendar. 'That's strange. It is almost exactly one year ago. I remember. It was late October. Maybe his ghost came back because he wanted to go home.' Richard and I looked at each other for a few seconds. He looked frightened. I felt frightened too. Richard put his coat on. 'And I want to go home. Come on, it's getting late.'

"I put my coat on and we locked the office door and walked out to our cars. A few months later, the bus company gave me a different bus route. I drove a bus on the other side of the town. Since then, I have seen the young man with the earphones, and the woman. Sometimes they get on my bus. But we never talk about that night. And I have never seen William since that night. Maybe he just wanted to go home. Maybe he wanted to go home for the last time."

"I want to go home too," said Pamela. "Has the snow stopped yet?"

They all looked out of the window. It was not snowing anymore. Then they heard the sound of an engine.

"It's the snow plough," said the bus driver. Soon they could see the lights of the snow plough. "We'll follow the snow plough."

He drove out of the car park and onto the road. The snow plough was pushing the snow to the side of the road. At first, they could only travel slowly, but then they came to a bigger road. The snow was not so deep there. The snow plough moved to the side of the road and the bus drove past it. Very soon they were near Boston.

The bus driver spoke again, "Look out the windows on the left side of the bus. Very soon we will pass the bus stop where William Vogel got on the bus and disappeared."

Everyone looked out the window. They looked at the bus stop by the side of the road.

"Did you see…?" said the bus driver.

No one answered him. No one wanted to say anything. They saw an old man standing next to the bus stop. The old man was wearing a red coat and a yellow baseball cap.

THANK YOU

Thank you for reading Stories for Halloween. (Word count: 8,679) We hope you enjoyed it.

If you would like to read more level 2 graded readers, please visit our website http://www.italkyoutalk.com

Other Level 2 graded readers include
Adventure in Rome
Andre's Dream
A Passion for Music
Christmas Tales
Danger in Seattle
Don't Come Back
Finders Keepers…
Marcy's Bakery
Men's Konkatsu Tales
Salaryman Secrets!
The Perfect Wedding
The House in the Forest
The School on Bolt Street
Train Travel
Trouble in Paris

Women's Konkatsu Tales

ABOUT THE AUTHOR

I Talk You Talk Press is a Japan-based publisher of language textbooks, graded readers and language learning/teaching resources.

Our team is made up of highly experienced language teachers and translators, who have all studied at least one additional language to an advanced level.

This experience enables us to design our materials from the perspective of both the teacher and the learner. We consult with both teachers and language learners when designing our textbooks and graded readers, and test our materials extensively in the classroom before publication.

We are a fast-growing press, and currently publish graded readers for learners of English. We publish new graded readers monthly.

www.ingramcontent.com/pod-product-compliance
Lightning Source LLC
Chambersburg PA
CBHW022350040426
42449CB00006B/815